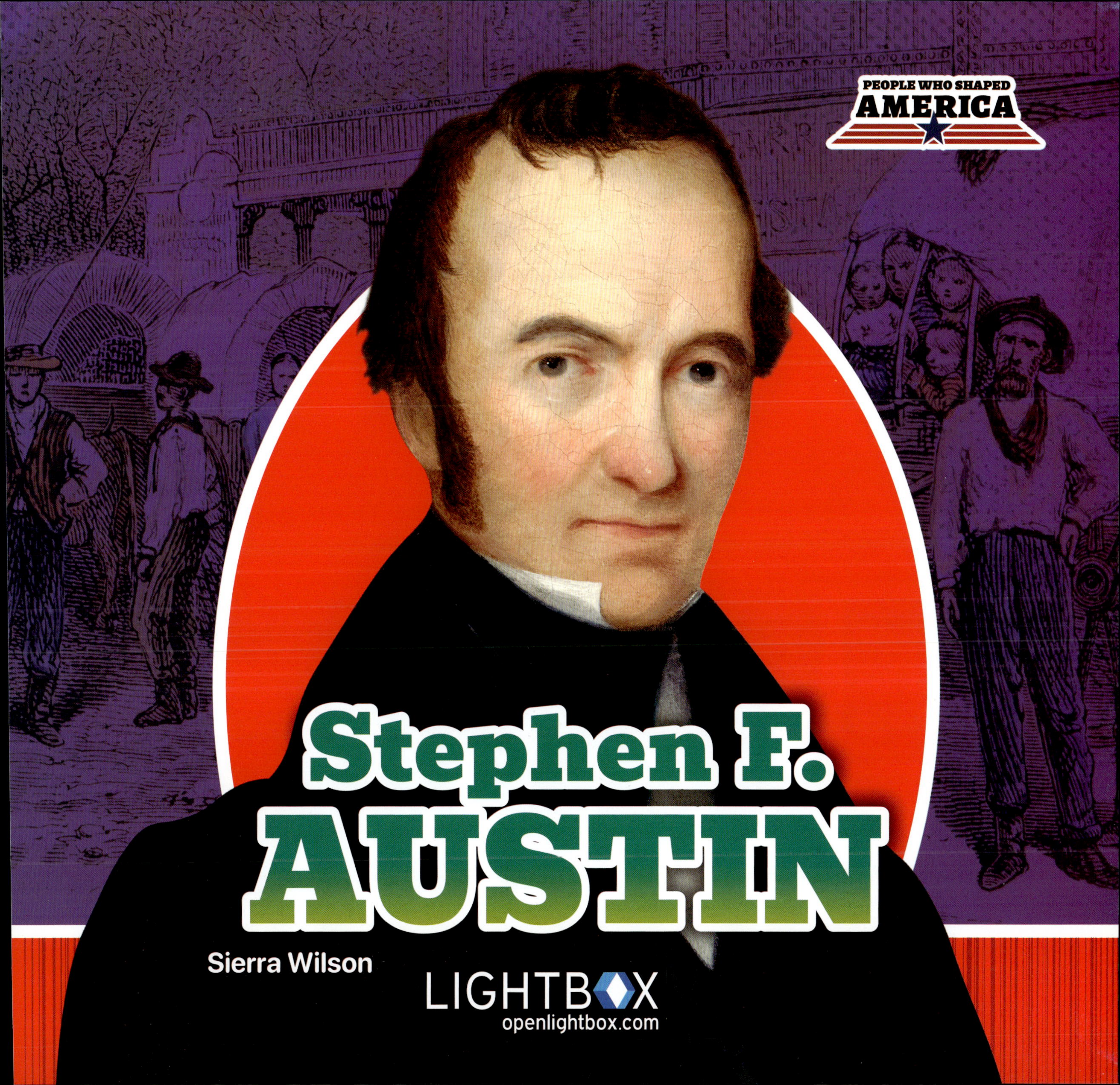

PEOPLE WHO SHAPED AMERICA

Stephen F. AUSTIN

Sierra Wilson

LIGHTBOX
openlightbox.com

LIGHTBOX

Go to **www.openlightbox.com** and enter this book's unique code.

ACCESS CODE

LBXF2737

Lightbox is an all-inclusive digital solution for the teaching and learning of curriculum topics in an original, groundbreaking way.

OPTIMIZED FOR

- ✓ TABLETS
- ✓ SMART BOARDS
- ✓ COMPUTERS
- ✓ AND MUCH MORE!

STANDARD FEATURES OF LIGHTBOX

- **AUDIO** High-quality narration using text-to-speech system
- **VIDEOS** Embedded high-definition video clips
- **ACTIVITIES** Printable PDFs that can be emailed and graded
- **WEBLINKS** Curated links to external, child-safe resources
- **SLIDESHOWS** Pictorial overviews of key concepts
- **INTERACTIVE MAPS** Interactive maps and aerial satellite imagery
- **QUIZZES** Ten multiple choice questions that are automatically graded and emailed for teacher assessment
- **KEY WORDS** Matching key concepts to their definitions

SUPPLEMENTARY RESOURCES

- **SHARE** Share titles within your Learning Management System (LMS) or Library Circulation System
- **CURRICULUM** Find national and state curriculum correlations
- **CITATION** Create bibliographical references following APA, CMSO, and MLA styles

VIDEOS

WEBLINKS

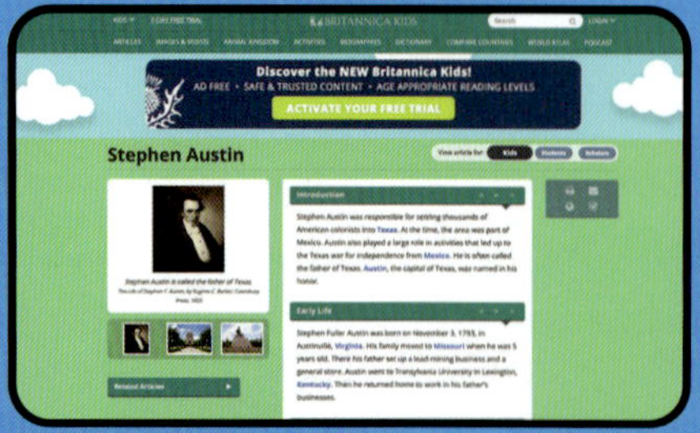

SLIDESHOWS

QUIZZES

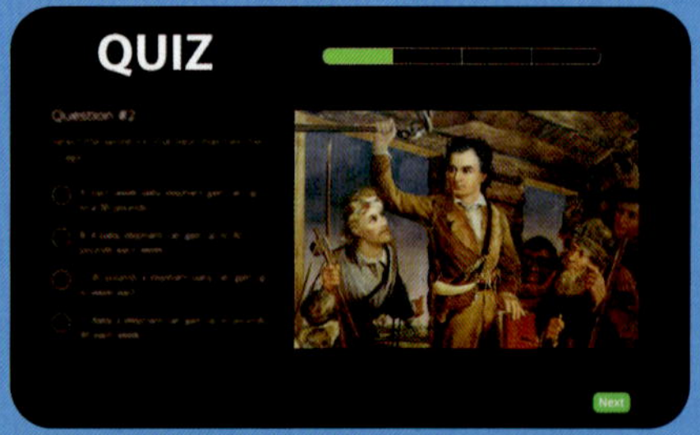

This title is part of our Lightbox digital subscription

1-Year Texas Subscription
978-1-5105-8659-8

Access hundreds of Lightbox titles with our digital subscription.
Sign up for a **FREE** subscription trial at **www.openlightbox.com/trial**

The digital components of this book are guaranteed to stay active for at least five years from the date of publication.

Stephen F. AUSTIN

CONTENTS

2 Lightbox Access Code
4 Who Was Stephen F. Austin?
6 Growing Up
8 Overcoming Obstacles
10 Character
12 Helping Others
14 Thoughts from Stephen
16 Leader
18 Achievements and Successes
20 Stephen F. Austin's Timeline
22 Cause and Effect
24 Key Words

Who Was Stephen F. Austin?

Stephen Fuller Austin worked to set up the first American settlement in Texas. Today, he is often called the "Father of Texas."

Stephen started his first settlement in **1821**.

STATE
TEXAS
Compiled from the records of the General Land Office of the State by
1856.

Growing Up

Stephen was born in Virginia in 1793. His father owned a mining company. When Stephen was 5 years old, the family moved to Missouri.

Stephen was put in charge of his father's mine when he was just **23 years old**.

Overcoming Obstacles

When Stephen was 27 years old, his father died. Stephen took over his father's dream of starting a settlement in Texas.

SAN FELIPE

Character

Stephen was known as a skilled leader. He was patient and worked hard. People trusted him.

Helping Others

Stephen set up five different settlements in Texas. He helped more than 1,500 families move there.

Thoughts from Stephen

Stephen spent much of his life helping Texas succeed. He believed it was a great place to live.

"The prosperity of Texas has been the object of my labors."

- Stephen F. Austin

Leader

Texas was part of Mexico in 1821. Stephen made many deals with Mexico's government. These deals helped Texas grow.

By 1832, more than 8,000 people were living in Stephen's settlements.

LIBERTY OR DEATH

Achievements and Successes

Stephen believed that Texas should leave Mexico. He worked to help it become independent. In 1836, Texas became a country of its own.

Austin has been the capital city of Texas since 1839. It was named in honor of Stephen.

Stephen F. Austin Timeline

1793
Born in Virginia

1798
Moves to Missouri with his family

1816
Begins managing his father's mines

1821
Starts his first Texas settlement

1832
Stephen's settlements have more than 8,000 residents

1836
Becomes Texas's Secretary of State

1836
Dies of pneumonia

1839
City of Austin becomes capital of Texas

2023
San Felipe, capital of Stephen's first settlement, celebrates its 200th birthday.

Cause and Effect

Cause

Stephen was a hard-working leader.

Effect

He was able to develop successful settlements in Texas.

Cause

Stephen believed Texas should leave Mexico.

Effect

He worked to help Texas gain its independence.

KEY WORDS

Research has shown that as much as 65 percent of all written material published in English is made up of 300 words. These 300 words cannot be taught using pictures or learned by sounding them out. They must be recognized by sight. This book contains 63 common sight words to help young readers improve their reading fluency and comprehension. This book also teaches young readers several important content words, such as proper nouns. These words are paired with pictures to aid in learning and improve understanding.

Page	Sight Words First Appearance
4	American, father, first, he, his, in, is, of, often, set, started, the, to, up, was, who
7	a, family, just, old, put, when, years
8	over, took
11	and, as, hard, him, people
12	different, more, move, others, than, there
15	been, from, great, has, it, life, live, much, my, place, thoughts
16	by, grow, made, many, part, these, were, with
19	city, country, help, its, leave, own, should, that

Page	Content Words First Appearance
4	settlement, Stephen Fuller Austin, Texas
7	company, mine, Missouri, Virginia
8	dream, obstacles
11	character, leader
15	labors, object, prosperity
16	deals, government, Mexico
19	achievements, honor, successes

Published by Lightbox Learning Inc.
276 5th Avenue, Suite 704 #917
New York, NY 10001
Website: www.openlightbox.com

Library of Congress Control Number: 2024933868

ISBN 978-1-5105-8386-3 (hardcover)
ISBN 978-1-5105-8387-0 (static multi-user eBook)
ISBN 978-1-5105-8389-4 (interactive multi-user eBook)

Printed in Guangzhou, China
1 2 3 4 5 6 7 8 9 0 28 27 26 25 24

052024
110823

Project Coordinator: Heather Kissock
Designer: Terry Paulhus
Layout: Jean Faye Rodriguez

Every reasonable effort has been made to trace ownership and to obtain permission to reprint copyright material. The publisher would be pleased to have any errors or omissions brought to its attention so that they may be corrected in subsequent printings.

The publisher acknowledges Getty Images, Alamy, Bridgeman Images, Shutterstock, and Wikimedia Commons as its primary image suppliers for this title.